THE
CHANGING
WORLD OF
RETIREMENT
PLANNING

WORKBOOK 1

WORKBOOK 1

THE CHANGING WORLD OF RETIREMENT PLANNING

Typesetting by *Wordzworth.com*

Contents

Estate Planning

Maximizing Social Security

SECTION ONE

Retiring in the 21st Century

Introduction

Everyone wants something different from retirement. No one person's retirement is going to look exactly like another's. Your greatest challenge may be to identify what *you* want most out of this new chapter of your life.

In this workshop, we will:

1. Review "traditional" retirement paradigms

2. Identify new paradigms and discuss how they affect you

3. Help you build a plan to get the most out of your retirement

The Old Paradigm

Approaching retirement like your parents approached it may not yield the best results. By contrasting the old retirement paradigm with the new retirement paradigm, you may be better prepared to get the most out of your retirement years.

Your parents' retirement may have consisted of the following:

- Work for the same company their whole career

- Retire at 65 and receive a pension

- Pension covered most lifestyle expenses

- Rely upon Social Security only for supplemental income

- Put less emphasis on one's own investments

The New Paradigm

Your parents wouldn't recognize the world of retirement planning into which most retirees are now venturing. How do you chart a course in this changing world of retirement planning? Retirees these days need a plan more than ever. Your retirement will likely be much different than that of your parents.

The following are a few reasons why:

- Average person now works for 7 different companies during career
- The 401(k) replaced the pension for many
- Retirement for many is mostly self-funded
- Social Security may cover very little of lifestyle requirements
- Some never fully retire but choose to stay engaged at some level.

Summary

- It's as important to know what you're retiring to as it is what you're retiring from

- Your retirement will likely look much different than the generation that came before you

- You will have to adopt updated paradigms as you plan your retirement

Throughout this course we will identify some of the new "paradigms" facing a new generation of retirees. Navigating these new paradigms will be critical to the success of your retirement in the 21st century.

SECTION TWO
Tax Rate Risk

Introduction

Many Americans have saved the lion's share of their retirement in tax-deferred accounts like 401(k)s and IRAs because of the perceived tax advantages. Today, however, we are marching into a future where our nation's debt load is at an all-time high and threatening to spiral out of control. What does this hold for the future of tax rates in America? If tax rates go up, how will this impact your cash flow in retirement?

In this section we will discuss the following:

- Why tax rates could double
- How our nation's debt may force tax rates to rise over time
- The extent to which our nation's entitlement programs are underfunded
- How rising tax rates may affect your cash flow in retirement
- How lost deductions may affect your tax burden in retirement

The Old Paradigm

The "old" tax paradigm as it relates to retirement planning states that:

- You will be living on less income in retirement

- You will therefore be in a lower tax bracket

- Given this lower tax bracket, tax-deferred investing is the best

Mathematically speaking, if you're going to be in a lower tax bracket in retirement, it makes sense to invest the vast majority of your retirement dollars in tax-deferred accounts like 401(k)s and IRAs. But will you *really* be in a lower tax bracket in retirement?

The New Paradigm

The "new" tax paradigm says that, in all actuality, your tax bracket in retirement may be higher than it is today.

This may be for a number of different reasons:

- You may need just as much income in retirement as you did during your working years
- Your marginal tax bracket may rise due to our country's fiscal challenges
- You may lose many of your greatest tax deductions in retirement

Where Did My Deductions Go?

Many of the deductions you experienced during your working years vanish right when you need them the very most: at retirement. The following are some of the larger deductions you may lose by the time you reach retirement:

- Interest on your mortgage
- Qualified retirement plan contributions (401k, 403b, etc.)
- Children – Tax Credit, Exemption
- Charity – many retirees donate time, not money

Many of these deductions during your working years may have added up to anywhere from $40,000 to $70,000.

Typical Deductions in Retirement

Absent these traditional deductions in retirement, most retirees are left with the following:

- Standard Deduction ($12,700)
- Personal Exemptions ($4,050 per person)

Because of this loss of deductions, it is possible to be in a higher tax bracket in retirement while living on less income.

A Brief History of Tax Rates

It's important to understand the history of tax rates so that we recognize that tax rates today are likely as low as we'll experience in our lifetime. Given our country's fiscal challenges, how much longer can we enjoy historically low tax rates?

Top marginal tax rates

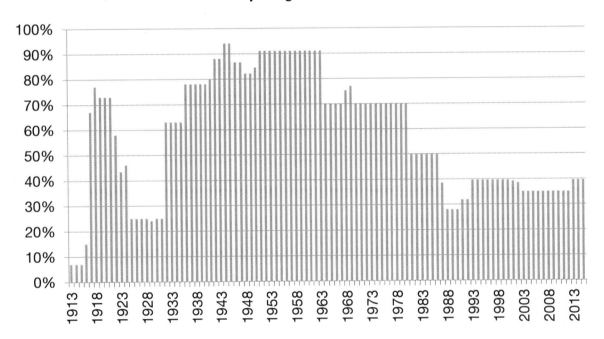

Source: Eugene Steuerle, The Urban Institute; Joseph Pechman, Federal Tax Policy; Joint Committee on taxation, Summary of Conference Agreement on the Jobs and Growth Tax Relief Reconciliation Act of 2003, JCx-54-03, May 22, 2003; IRS Revised Tax Rate Schedule

Highlights:

- The last two years of World War II, the highest marginal tax bracket was 94%

- Throughout the entire decade of the 70s, taxes hovered around 70%

- In 2012, the highest tax bracket was 35%, historically low

Are Taxes Going Up or Down?

As we move forward in time, to 2020, 2025 and beyond, will tax rates be higher or lower than they are today? The following are a few factors that (absent a dramatic reduction in spending) could force tax rates to rise:

- Social Security

- Medicare and Medicaid

- Interest on the National Debt

- Fannie Mae and Freddie Mac

- Department of Defense

- The Prescription Drug Program for Seniors

- Pension Obligations

- Etc.

Many of these are what the government calls "unfunded liabilities". An unfunded liability is a promise the government has made that it has no way of honoring. Some calculations put these total unfunded obligations at close to $120 trillion![1]

---

[1] nypost.com/2011/06/26/120-trillion-the-shocking-true-size-of-our-nations-debt/

What Are Our Country's Biggest Expenses?

Which of the aforementioned "unfunded liabilities" will, if not addressed, be the greatest contributors to our nation's increased debt load?

- Social Security
- Medicare and Medicaid

As of 2016, 66% of every tax dollar that comes into the US Treasury goes to pay for only four things:

- Social Security
- Medicare
- Medicaid
- Interest on our national debt

As Baby Boomers leave the work force and move onto the roles of entitlement programs, this landscape will begin to change. By 2020, those 4 expenses will consume 92% of all tax revenue flowing into the US Treasury.[2] This leaves 8 cents of every tax dollar to pay for everything else! Let's take a look at what "everything else" entails:

---

[2] https://www.nationalpriorities.org/analysis/2014/presidents-2015-budget-in-pictures, http://money.cnn.com/2011/01/21/news/economy/spending_taxes_debt/index.htm.

Children's nutrition, Border Security, Food Safety and Inspection Service, disaster relief, U.S. Forest Service, Drug Enforcement Administration, Public Housing Program, IRS, Animal and Plant Health Inspection, federal courts, Bureau of Indian Affairs, NASA, Army, National Endorsement for the Arts, Air Force, federal student loans, Rural Development, Coast Guard, Food Stamps, National Park Service, income assistance, Department of Family Services, research and development, U.S. Geological Survey, Environmental Protection Agency, Centers for Disease Control and Prevention, FEMA, Immigration and Customs Enforcement, Secret Service, FAA, Supportive Housing for the Elderly Program, Federal Railroad Administration, Navy, Bureau of Land Management, federal pension system, Peace Corps, FCC, State Department, National Science Foundation, Congress, Fish and Wildlife Service, White House, SEC, Smithsonian Institute, Small Business Administration, FBI, Federal Highway Administration...[3]

---

[3] http://money.cnn.com/2011/01/21/news/economy/spending_taxes_debt/index.htm.

Will Taxes Go Up?

David Walker

David Walker was the Comptroller General of the federal government from 1997 to 2008 under Presidents Bush and Clinton. He was the head of the Government Accountability Office (GAO), and served on the board of Social Security for 7 years. He may know more about our country's fiscal condition than anyone. He said this about the prospect of higher taxes:

> *"Regardless of what politicians tell you, any additional accumulations of debt are, absent dramatic reductions in the size and role of government, basically deferred tax increases...Unless we begin to get our fiscal house in order, there's simply no other way to handle our ever-mounting debt burdens except by doubling taxes over time."*[4]

---

[4] David Walker, "Commentary: Why Your Taxes Could Double", CNN.com, April 15, 2009, http://www.cnn.com/2009/POLITICS/04/15/walker.tax.debt/

Forbes Magazine

Here's what Forbes magazine had to say about taxing the rich as a means of solving our nation's fiscal crisis:

"The problem is that there are not enough 'high income earners' to satisfy today's debt and deficits. This means that middle income America will soon be in the scope of the Congressional rifle...Because the poor have nothing to tax, the middle class will be forced to ante up."[5]

The Congressional Budget Office

Finally, in 2008, the Congressional Budget Office (CBO) was asked to project how high tax rates would have to go to pay for Social Security, Medicare, and Medicaid. This is what they said:

"If Social Security, Medicare and Medicaid go unchanged, the rate for the lowest bracket would increase from 10% to 25%; the tax rate on incomes in the current 25% bracket would have to be increased to 63%; and the tax rate of the highest bracket would have to be raised from 35% to 88%."

---

[5] http://www.cbo.gov/ftpdocs/92xx/doc9216/05-19-LongtermBudget_Letter-to-Ryan.pdf

Historical Precedence

Before we explore the possibility of *higher* tax rates in the future, let's remind ourselves of how low tax rates are today. Our tax system in our country works in the following way. Some of your money is taxed at 10%, some at 15, some at 25, some at 28, some at 33, some at 35, and some at 39.6%.

2017	10%	15%	25%	28%	33%	35%	39.6%

According to the CBO, absent any reduction in spending, these are the levels to which tax rates would have to rise to keep our country solvent:

Future	25%	63%	88%

Many are skeptical when faced with the prospect of higher tax rates. You don't have to go very far back in the history of our country, however, to find tax rates that were that high. From 1960 to 1963, tax rates in our country were the following:

1960–63	26%	38%	56%	69%	78%	87%

There is historical precedence to suggest that tax rates in the future could rise, and in dramatic fashion.

Could Tax Rates Really Double?

Tax Rates Around the World

We are one of the only industrialized nations in the world that doesn't have tax rates that approach the 50% mark.[6]

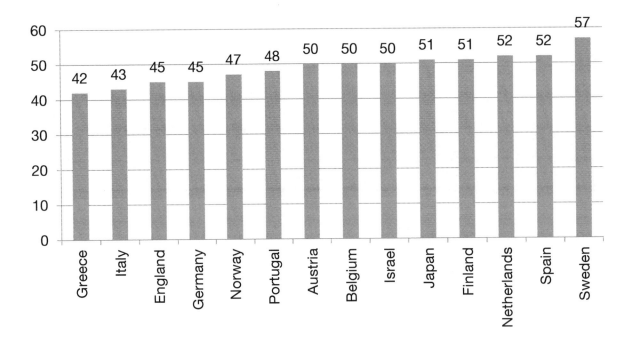

The math suggests that, absent any spending cuts, we may soon be joining the ranks of countries around the world whose tax rates are at or above 50%.

[6] http://www.kpmg.com/global/en/services/tax/tax-tools-and-resources/pages/individual-income-tax-rates-table.aspx

U.S. Debt vs. Interest on Debt

In the Year 2000

In the year 2000, our national debt was $5.6 Trillion, yet the cost of servicing that debt was an astounding $222 Billion.

In the Year 2017

Today, our national debt is $20 Trillion. Yet, when we look at the annual interest we're paying on that $20 Trillion, it's about $257 Billion. That's only $35 Billion more than what we were paying 17 years ago when the debt was less than a third as much as it is today.[7]

Why is the Cost of Debt Service in 2000 & 2017 the same?

The reason it costs lest to service debt today is because of one simple fact: interest rates today are at historically low levels. They have never been this low for this long. If interest rates were to return to historically normal levels, what would happen to the cost to service our national debt on an annual basis? It would more than triple!

For that reason, even if we somehow solved the underfunding problems associated with Social Security, Medicare and Medicaid, we could still have a major problem with our $20 Trillion dollar national debt. If interest rates rise to normal levels, our government may have no other choice but to raise taxes.

[7] Usdebtclock.org

In Summary

In this section we learned that:

- Absent dramatic and permanent spending cuts, tax rates in the future are likely to be much higher than they are today

- There is historical precedence for higher taxes

- You will not likely have as many deductions in retirement as you did during your working years

- Retirement accounts like 401(k)s and IRAs may be exposed to inordinate amounts of tax rate risk

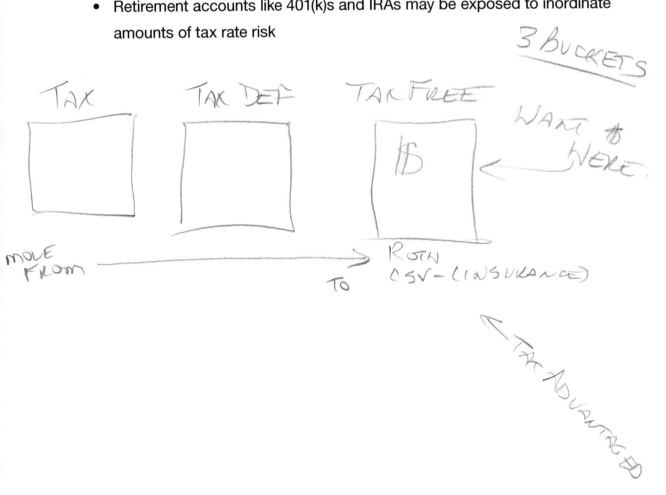

SECTION THREE

Retirement Distribution Planning

Introduction

Accumulating dollars in the right types of accounts can be just as important as growing them in the right investments. In this section we will cover the following:

- The three basic types of retirement accounts

- How to contribute to these accounts in order to maximize cash flow in retirement

- What's better: tax-deferred, tax-advantaged or both?

- How to define a "true" tax-advantaged investment

- When you should convert your IRA to a Roth IRA

- How distributions from IRAs and 401(k)s affect Social Security taxation

- Strategies to reduce or eliminate taxes in retirement

The Old Paradigm

The old retirement paradigm always worked under the premise that your taxes were going to be substantially lower in retirement than during your working years. In this case, it made sense to accumulate the lion's share of your assets in tax-deferred accounts. The thinking was, get a deduction at higher tax rates in order to postpone the payment of those taxes until much later in life when your tax rate was likely to be lower.

The New Paradigm

Your tax picture during your retirement may differ from that of your parents in the following ways:

- You may need as much income in your retirement years as you did during your working years

- Our country's fiscal challenges may force tax rates higher

- You may lose many of your greatest tax deductions in retirement

- You may be in a higher tax bracket in retirement than you were during your working years

- Accumulating dollars thoughtfully and proactively in a variety of retirement accounts may extend the life of your retirement assets

What is Retirement Distribution Planning?

Retirement Distribution Planning can be defined as the following:

"Accumulating the right amount of money in the right types of accounts in order to maximize cash flow in retirement."

The 3 Types of Investment Accounts

There are many different types of investments that you can utilize to save for retirement. However, all of those investments fit into only three basic types of accounts. During this course, we will refer to these accounts as buckets of money. They are as follows:

- The Taxable Bucket

- The Tax-Deferred Bucket

- The Tax-Advantaged Bucket

If tax rates in the future are likely to be higher than they are today, then we need to be very thoughtful and intentional about how we accumulate dollars in these types of accounts. Failing to do so may cause us to pay hundreds of thousands of dollars in avoidable taxes in retirement.

ROTH CONVERSION CAN OCCUR FROM ANY ACCOUNT THAT YOU CAN ROLL MONEY FROM INTO ROTH.

To better understand the importance of accumulating the right amounts of money in the right types of accounts, let's begin by identifying the pros and cons of each bucket.

The Taxable Bucket

In this bucket, you pay taxes if your money grows, regardless of whether you take money out. The following are a few examples of taxable investments:

- Savings Accounts
- Money Markets
- CDs
- Mutual Funds
- Stocks
- Bonds
- Etc.

The tipoff that you have taxable investments is the 1099 you receive from your financial institution at the end of each year. The 1099 reports to the IRS the amount of taxable income you received from a given investment. The taxable bucket has pros and cons which help you understand how to best incorporate it into your retirement savings plan.

Pros

- Generally Liquid (accessible)[8]
- GENERALLY PRETTY SAFE

---

[8] The value of stocks, bonds and mutual funds can rise and fall with the market which may make them less liquid than other taxable alternatives

Cons

- Growth is taxable

- 1099s from these accounts may cause your Social Security to be taxed (more about this in Section 5)

Because taxable investments are generally liquid, the taxable bucket makes for a good emergency fund. It is generally recommended that you have 6 months' worth of living expenses in your emergency fund.[9]

Risks Associated with a Balance That Is Too Large

- Inflation risk (due to the low rates of return of some of the more traditional taxable accounts, i.e., CDs, money markets, savings, etc.)

- Tax inefficiency

- The Double Compounding Problem

[9] The value of stocks, bonds and mutual funds can rise and fall with the market which may make them less liquid than other taxable alternatives

The Double Compounding Problem

The Double Compounding Problem occurs when you grow your money in your taxable bucket while tax rates rise steadily over time.

Consider this example: Let's say that you make a contribution of $100,000 to a taxable investment which earns 5% per year. Because this investment is taxable, you would pay tax at your marginal tax rate, both federal and state (if applicable). In this example, we'll use 25% federal and 5% state tax for a total of 30%. By the end of the first year, your pre-tax investment return is $5,000. But when we figure in taxes at the 30% rate, your true after-tax return is only $3,500.

In the following chart, we continue down this road for 10 years, raising taxes by 1% with each passing year. By the 10th year, you can see the true impact of this double compounding effect: a 74% increase in your tax bill!

Year	Combined Federal and State Tax Rate	Annual Balance	Pre-tax Investment Income at 5% Growth	After-tax Investment Income	Total Tax Bill
1	30%	$100,000	$5,000	$3,500	$1,500
2	31%	$103,500	$5,175	$3,571	$1,604
3	32%	$107,071	$5,354	$3,640	$1,713
4	33%	$110,711	$5,536	$3,709	$1,827
5	34%	$114,420	$5,721	$3,776	$1,945
6	35%	$118,196	$5,910	$3,841	$2,068
7	36%	$122,037	$6,102	$3,905	$2,197
8	37%	$125,942	$6,297	$3,967	$2,330
9	38%	$129,910	$6,495	$4,027	$2,468
10	39%	$133,937	$6,697	$4,085	$2,612

DON'T WANT TO KEEP MONEY IN TAXABLE BUCKET. WANT IT IN TAX-FREE - GROWS FASTER!

Comparison: Taxable vs. Tax-Advantaged

By comparing a taxable investment to a tax-advantaged alternative, we can better understand the dangers of accumulating too much money in the taxable bucket over time.

Example

- An investor contributes $6,500 to each account
- Each account grows at 8%[10]
- Taxable account is taxed at 31%
    - Federal Tax: 25%
    - State Tax: 6%[11]
- Both accounts grow for 30 years[12]

Let's see what happens if we grow these two accounts side-by-side over the course of a 30 year retirement.[13]

---

[10] Assumed rates of return are not guaranteed
[11] Tax rates may vary depending on the state of residence
[12] Investors should consider current and anticipated investment horizon and income tax bracket when making a decision
[13] This example is for illustrative purposes only and is not a solicitation or recommendation of any investment strategy or product

Comparison: Taxable vs. Tax-Advantaged

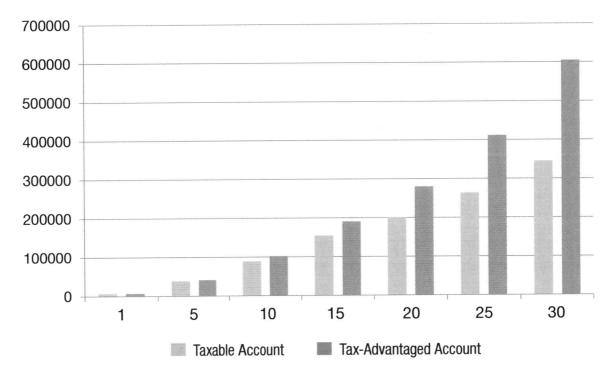

Taxable Account   Tax-Advantaged Account

In review, because of the inherent tax-inefficiency of the taxable bucket, the ideal balance to have is about 6 months' worth of basic living expenses.

You may have more than 6 months' in your taxable bucket, so long as you recognize that it comes at a price. In this example, that cost was about $300,000 over a 30 year time frame.

The Tax-Deferred Bucket

With the tax-deferred bucket, you don't pay taxes as your money grows. You do, however, pay taxes in retirement upon distribution. The following are examples of tax-deferred investments:

- 401(k)

- IRA

- 403(b)

- 457

- Simple IRA

- SEP

These types of plans generally have two things in common:

1. Contributions are *tax deductible*: For example, if you make $100,000 and put $10,000 into your 401(k), your taxable income reduces to $90,000.

2. Distributions are taxed as *ordinary income*: For example, when you contribute money to your 401(k), you defer the receipt of that income until distribution in retirement. At what rate are you taxed? Whatever the tax rate happens to be in the year you make the distribution.

Other Caveats

- Distributions may cause your Social Security to be taxed (more in Section 5)

- 10% penalty for distributions before age 59 ½

- Required Minimum Distributions (RMDs) begin at age 70 ½

Required Minimum Distributions

With your RMDs, the IRS forces you to take distributions at age 70 ½. Those distributions start out at 3.65% of your cumulative tax-deferred accounts and get bigger every year. The chart below shows your RMDs year by year:[14]

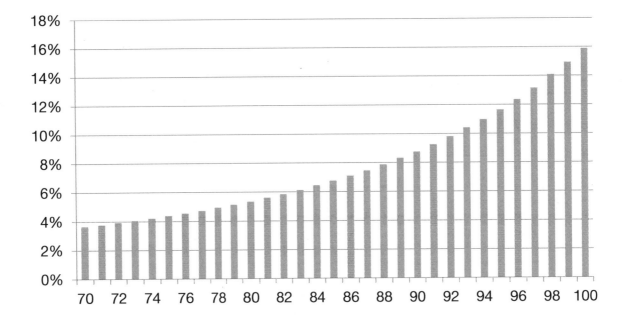

These increasing RMDs may have unintended consequences as it relates to your overall tax burden in retirement as well as affect Social Security taxation. There will be more discussion on the implications of Social Security taxation in Section 5.

[14] http://www.forbes.com/sites/baldwin/2014/03/17/rmd-tables-for-iras/

The Changing World of Retirement Planning

Benefits of Tax-Deferred Investing

If you believe that your tax rate in retirement is likely to be higher than it is today, then there are some good rules of thumb to follow when it comes to tax-deferred investing.

1. Contribute to your 401(k) up to the match, but not above and beyond.

2. Keep your tax-deferred balances low enough so that RMDs in retirement are equal to or less than your Standard Deductions and Personal Exemptions.

Rule of thumb #2 requires some explanation. Most people have very few if any deductions left by the time they retire. If that's the case the IRS does give you some deductions. They are as follows:

- Standard Deduction: $12,700

- Personal Exemption: $4,050 ($8,100 for a married couple)

Example

@ 70½ - ARE 3.65% OF IRA BALANCE

If you were taking RMDs this year (2017), you would want your tax-deferred balances to be low enough that your RMDs would be equal to or less than your standard deductions plus personal exemptions. In that case, you would want your RMDs to be no greater than $20,800.

Given an IRA balance of $500,000 and given an initial RMD rate of 3.65%, your RMD would be $18,250. In this case your RMDs would be free from tax. This turns your tax-deferred vehicles into an ideal investment. You experienced a deduction upon contribution, your money grew tax-deferred, and you took it out without paying tax. This scenario illustrates one of the true benefits of tax-deferred investing.[15]

If, on the other hand, your tax-deferred balances were $1,000,000, your RMDs would be $36,500, much greater than your actual deductions. This would expose a portion of your RMDs to the ebb and flow of tax rates over time.

The Moral of the Story

When you have too much money in your tax-deferred bucket, you may expose yourself to higher tax rates in the future making it much more difficult to have a tax-efficient retirement.

[15] RMDs this high may cause Social Security taxation. See Chapter 5 for a full discussion of Provisional Income

The Tax-Advantaged Bucket

Before we get into the attributes of the tax-advantaged bucket, we must first acknowledge that there are investments that have every appearance of being tax-advantaged, but that fall short in a number of ways. Here are a few:

- Municipal Bonds
- Oil and Gas Partnerships

To qualify as tax-advantaged, an investment must embody the following attributes:

- Free from all taxes (Federal, State and Capital Gains)
- Distributions do not cause Social Security to be taxed

Examples of Tax-Advantaged Investments:

- Roth IRAs
- Roth 401(k)s
- Roth Conversions
- Some properly structured cash value life insurance policies

The Roth IRA

So long as you are at least 59 ½ when you take money out of your Roth IRA you don't pay any of the three taxes mentioned above. Second, when you take distributions from your Roth IRA, it does not count against the thresholds that cause your Social Security to be taxed.

Other attributes of the Roth IRA are as follows:

- Contribution limit: $5,500 per person
- Catch-up Provision: $6,500 per person after age 50
- Principal is liquid from day 1
- To avoid penalty on growth, you must be 59 ½ *and* have held the Roth IRA for 5 years
- To qualify for the Roth IRA, you must meet the IRS's income parameters

Income Parameters

- Married Filing Jointly: Phase out begins at $186,000 and ends at $195,999
- Single Filers: Phase out begins at $118,000 and ends at $132,999

Also, you can only contribute to a Roth IRA if you have earned income. To fully max out your Roth IRAs, you must have earned income equal to or greater than the contributions.

For example: If your adjusted gross income were $8,000, you could contribute a maximum of $8,000 to your and your spouse's cumulative Roth IRAs.

If your adjusted gross income were $15,000, you could contribute the full $13,000 to your Roth IRAs.

The Roth 401(k):

Many companies these days have the Roth 401(k), but few advertise it. To find out if your company has one, talk to your human resources department. The Roth 401(k) is powerful because it allows you to make huge contributions to your tax-advantaged bucket on an annual basis. The contribution limits of the Roth 401(k) are:

- Contribution limit: $18,000 per year
- Catch-up Provision: $24,000 per year

Tax-Deferred or Tax-Advantaged?

So, it's probably a good time to ask the question: Should you contribute your money to tax-deferred accounts or tax-advantaged accounts? Should you pay tax on the seed or should you pay tax on the harvest? Should you do a Traditional 401(k) or a Roth 401(k)?

Now, there are all sorts of online calculators that profess to be able to tell you which one is better, but only one factor determines which account you should be doing, and it's this: Do you think your tax bracket in the future will be higher or lower than it is today?

Roth IRA vs. Traditional IRA

This diagram will help you determine whether you should invest in tax-deferred or tax-advantaged accounts for retirement. It shouldn't be any more complicated than this. Let's assume that your tax rate today is 25%. If that's the case then only one of three things can happen to that tax rate during your retirement. It can either go up, go down, or stay the same.

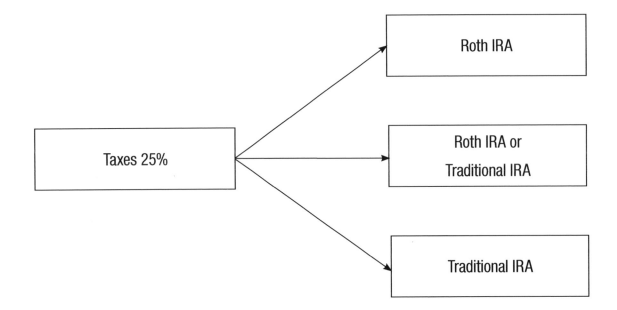

- If your tax rate goes up, then mathematically you'll be better off doing a Roth IRA

- If your tax rate goes down, you're better off doing a Traditional IRA

- If your tax rate stays the same, it doesn't really matter which one you do, because you'll have the same after-tax cash flow in either one

The Story of Twin Brothers Doug and Gary

You may have heard the argument that Roth IRAs are deficient because you're contributing after-tax dollars. This argument suggests that since you are contributing after-tax dollars, you aren't able to contribute as much and, therefore, won't have as much money over the long-term. Let's use a little math to debunk this financial myth.

Again, the only determining factor in whether you should contribute to a Roth IRA is what you think your tax rate will be when you retire. Case closed, end of story. Let's illustrate this with the example of twin brothers Gary and Doug, both age 35.[16]

Gary is in a 30% tax bracket and likes the idea of tax deductions, so he opts for the tax-deferred approach. He decides to put $5,000 of pretax dollars in his Traditional IRA each year. He then lets those contributions grow and compound for the next 30 years. By the time he retires at age 65, he has $611,729 in his IRA. Only he doesn't really have that much because he hasn't paid taxes yet. Remember, the only dollars that really matter are those which we can spend after tax, right? Let's also assume that tax rates when Gary is 65 (suspending belief for just a moment) are still at 30%. How much of that $611,729 is left after tax, assuming that he pays tax on all distributions? The answer is $428,211.

Gary's brother Doug opts for the tax-advantaged approach with his Roth IRA. Because he's contributing dollars that have already been taxed at 30%, he can now only invest $3,500 per year. He grows these dollars over the same period of time, and then decides to retire at age 65. How much money will he have? The answer may suprise you: $428,211. It's the same as Gary, down to the last red penny.

[16] This example is for illustrative purposes only and is not a solicitation or recommendation of any investment strategy or product.

Traditional IRA vs. Roth IRA
Ending Balances with Same Tax Rate and Higher Future Rate

	No Change in Tax Rate		1% Increase in Tax Rate	
	Gary	Doug	Gary	Doug
Vehicle	Traditional IRA	Roth IRA	Traditional IRA	Roth IRA
Contribution Per Year	$5,000	$5,000	$5,000	$5,000
Tax Rate at Age 35	30%	30%	30%	30%
After-Tax Contribution Per Year	$5,000	$3,500	$5,000	$3,500
Average Rate of Return Per Year for 30 Years	8%	8%	8%	8%
End Value of Investment at Age 65	$611,729	$428,211	$611,729	$428,211
Tax Rate at Age 65	30%	30%	31%	31%
After-Tax End Value	$428,211	$428,211	$422,093	$428,211

What's the moral of the story? If tax rates in the future are the same as they are today, it doesn't matter which IRA you choose, Roth or Traditional. However, if tax rates in the future are just one percent higher, you're better off choosing the Roth IRA. In Gary's case, 1% higher taxes means he's left with only $422,093, in which case Doug wins!

In order to figure out which type of account to invest in, you have to ask yourself what you truly believe about the future of tax rates.

The Ideal Amount in the Tax-Advantaged Bucket

If tax rates in the future are likely to be higher than they are today, there is an ideal amount to have in your tax-advantaged bucket.

- Everything above and beyond the ideal amounts in the taxable bucket (more than 6 months) should be shifted to tax-advantaged

- Everything above and beyond the ideal amounts in the tax-deferred bucket (RMDs equal to or less than standard deductions and personal exemptions in retirement) should be shifted to tax-advantaged[17]

Remember, that's only if you think that tax rates in the future will be higher than they are today. So, again, you really have to ask yourself where you think tax rates will be in the year you take these dollars out.

---

[17] To avoid Social Security taxation, balances in the tax-deferred bucket may need to be further reduced to stay below Provisional Income thresholds. See Chapter 5 for a full discussion of Provisional Income

In Summary

If taxes in the future are likely to be higher than they are today, then we have to be very thoughtful about where we choose to grow and compound our retirement savings. As we prepare for a retirement with an eye towards tax efficiency, we must keep in mind the following:

- There are three basic types of accounts in which to save for retirement: taxable, tax-deferred and tax-advantaged

- If taxes are likely to be higher in the future, there is a mathematically ideal amount to have in each account or "bucket"

- The Taxable Bucket should have 6 months' worth of basic income needs

- The Tax-Deferred Bucket should have a low enough balance that RMDs can be offset by standard deductions and personal exemptions

- The Tax-Advantaged bucket should hold anything above and beyond the ideal amounts in the taxable and tax-deferred buckets

- A true Tax-Advantaged investment is free from all 3 types of tax and does not contribute to the thresholds that cause Social Security taxation

SECTION FOUR

Estate Planning

Introduction

Estate planning isn't just about reducing your taxes. It's also about making sure your assets are distributed as you wish — both now and after you're gone. With that in mind, you need to consider four questions before you begin your estate planning... or reconsider them if you're reviewing your estate plan.

1. Who do you want to inherit your assets?

2. How should you transfer your property at death?

3. Should you use a will or a trust?

4. How do you plan to address incapacity due to illness, injury, etc.?

Who Should Inherit Your Assets?

Let's look at the first question — who should inherit your assets? If you're married, before you can decide who will inherit your assets, you must consider marital rights. For example, states have different laws designed to protect surviving spouses. If you die without a will or a living trust, state law will dictate how much passes to your spouse.

And even if you have a will or living trust, if you provide less for your spouse than your state's law deems appropriate, the law may very well allow the survivor to elect to receive the greater amount.

It's also critical that you consider whether your children should share equally in your estate and if you want to include your grandchildren or others as beneficiaries. And if you're charitably minded, you may want to leave some of your assets to charity.

Finally, if you live in a community property state or your estate includes community property, you'll need to consider the impact on your estate planning.

As you can see, there's a lot for you to consider...

Which Assets Should They Inherit?

There are some questions you should consider when transferring certain types of assets. For example, if you own a business, do you want the stock to pass only to your children who are actively involved in the business? If so, should you compensate the others with assets of comparable value?

Plus, if you own rental properties, should all of your beneficiaries inherit those properties? It's a tricky question, I know. But it's critical that you decide which of your heirs have the ability to manage the properties. And then you need to consider the cash needs of each beneficiary.

When and How Should They Inherit Assets?

When answering this question, you need to focus on the potential age and maturity of the beneficiaries and the financial needs of you and your spouse during your lifetimes. Finally, you'll need to consider all the tax implications.

Outright Bequests vs. Trusts

Let's take a look at the age-old debate of whether it's best to give outright bequests or to set up trusts. On the one hand, outright bequests offer simplicity, flexibility and some tax advantages. But on the other, you'll have no control over what the recipient does with the assets.

Trusts are more complex, but they can be useful if your heirs are young or immature or they lack asset management capabilities. Trusts also can help save taxes and protect assets from creditors.

Transferring Property at Death

Choices for Transferring Assets

There are several ways for your assets to be transferred on your death. The most common is a will, which is the standard method; then there's the living trust, which offers some advantages over a will; and finally, beneficiary designations, for assets such as life insurance and IRAs.

If you die without either a will or a living trust, state intestate succession law will control the disposition of your property that doesn't otherwise pass via "operation of law." An example of this is beneficiary designation. What's more, settling your estate likely will be more troublesome — and more costly. Bottom line? It's critical that you have either a will or a living trust in place.

You might be wondering about the difference between a will and a living trust. Basically, it's that assets placed in your living trust (except in rare circumstances) avoid probate at your death. So, neither the will nor the living trust document, in and of itself, reduces estate taxes — though both can be drafted to do this. Let's take a closer look at these options...

With a Will:

Now, if you choose just a will, it's highly likely that your estate will have to go through probate. Probate is a court-supervised process that protects the rights of creditors and beneficiaries, and it ensures the orderly and timely transfer of assets.

Probate can be quite advantageous, as it provides standardized procedures and court supervision. Also, the creditor claims limitation period is often shorter than for, say, a living trust.

The probate process typically includes six steps …

Step 1: Notification of Interested Parties

The first step is notifying interested parties, which typically include any beneficiaries named in the will, your natural heirs and, of course, any creditors.

Most states require disclosure of the estate's approximate value as well as the names and addresses of interested parties.

Step 2: Appointment of an Executor or Personal Representative

The second step in the probate process involves appointing an executor or personal representative. Hopefully, you have already appointed this person, but if not, the court will appoint one for you to oversee your estate's liquidation and distribution.

Step 3: Inventory of Assets

The third step consists of accounting for all the assets you owned or controlled at the time of your death.

Step 4: Payment of Claims

The fourth step is the payment of claims. The type and length of notice required to establish a deadline for creditors to file their claims vary by state. If a creditor doesn't file its claim on time, the claim will typically be barred.

Step 5: Filing of Tax Returns

Next, your executor needs to file the individual's final income taxes and the estate's income taxes. Finally ...

Step 6: Distribution of Residuary Estate

After the estate has paid all its debts and taxes, the executor or personal representative should distribute any remaining assets to the beneficiaries and then close the estate.

Now let's turn our attention to living trusts...

Living Trusts

Because probate is time-consuming, potentially expensive and public, avoiding it altogether is a common estate planning goal. A living trust — which is also known as a revocable trust, declaration of trust or inter vivos trust — acts as a will substitute.

But, you'll still need to have a short will, which is often referred to as a "pour over" will.

So, just how does a living trust work?

How Living Trusts Work

First, you transfer assets into a trust for your own benefit during your lifetime.

You can serve as trustee, select another individual to serve, or select a professional trustee. If you serve as trustee, the successor trustee you name will take over as trustee upon your death.

In nearly every state, you'll avoid probate if all of your assets are in the living trust when you die, or if any assets not in the trust are held in a manner that allows them to pass automatically by operation of law — for example, in a joint bank account. The pour over will can specify how assets you didn't transfer to your living trust during your life will be transferred at death.

Essentially, you retain the right to revoke the trust and appoint and remove trustees. If you name a professional trustee to manage trust assets, you can require the trustee to consult with you before buying or selling assets.

Finally, the trust doesn't need to file an income tax return until after you die. Instead, you pay the tax on any income the trust earns as if you had never created the trust.

Benefits of Living Trusts

A living trust offers additional benefits. First, your assets aren't exposed to public record. Besides keeping your affairs private, this makes it more difficult for anyone to challenge the disposition of your estate.

Second, a living trust can serve as a vehicle for managing your financial assets if you become incapacitated and unable to manage them yourself. We'll discuss planning for incapacity in more detail a little later in this presentation.

Keep in mind that only assets titled in your living trust's name avoid probate. So make sure you change the title of all assets you want managed by the trust.

Selecting an Executor, Personal Representative or Trustee

Whether you choose a will or a living trust, it's critical that you select someone to administer the disposition of your estate. This person will act as your executor or personal representative. If you have a living trust, this person will act as the trustee.

Some people want a family member, friend or professional advisor to take on this role. Others would rather assign this task to an institution, such as a bank or trust company.

Many people name both an individual and an institution to leverage their collective expertise.

Professional vs. Individual Trustee

Which should you choose? There are advantages of both a professional and an individual executor, personal representative or trustee.

Many people name a spouse, child or other relative to act as executor, personal representative, or trustee. That person can certainly hire any professional assistance, if needed.

There are other things you should consider as well. For example, you should make sure the executor, personal representative or trustee you name doesn't have a conflict of interest. You'll want to think twice about choosing a second spouse, children from a prior marriage, or an individual who owns part of your business. It's possible that the desires of a stepparent and stepchildren may conflict, and a co-owner's personal goals regarding your business may differ from those of your family.

Also make sure the executor, personal representative or trustee is willing to serve. The job isn't easy, and not everyone will want or accept the responsibility. Even if you choose an individual rather than a professional, consider paying a reasonable fee for the services. Finally, provide for an alternate in case your first choice is unable or unwilling to perform when the time comes.

Responsibilities of Executor, Personal Representative or Trustee

After all this talk of executors, trustees, and the like, you may wonder what in the world these people do?

He or she will serve after your death and will have several major responsibilities, including administering the estate and distributing assets to the beneficiaries. This person will also need to make certain tax decisions, pay the estate's debts or expenses and ensure life insurance and retirement plan benefits are received. Finally, this person will need to file the necessary tax returns and pay all taxes.

Selecting a Guardian for Your Children

If you have minor children, perhaps the most important element of your estate plan doesn't involve your assets. Rather, it involves who will be your children's guardian. Of course, the well-being of your children is your top priority, but there are some financial issues to consider.

For example, is the person capable of managing your children's assets? Can he or she afford to care for them? Will the home accommodate your children?

If you prefer, you can name separate guardians for your child and his or her assets. Taking the time to name a guardian or guardians now ensures your children will be cared for as you wish if you die while they're still minors.

Planning for Incapacity

It's also important that your estate plan address incapacity due to an illness, injury, advanced age or other circumstances.

Unless you specify how financial and health care decisions will be made in the event you become incapacitated, there's no guarantee your wishes will be carried out. And your family may have to go through expensive and time-consuming guardianship proceedings.

Let's review your estate planning options for making financial and health care decisions if you become incapacitated.

Making Financial Decisions

Two planning techniques to consider regarding making financial decisions while incapacitated are a durable power of attorney and a living trust.

Durable Power of Attorney

A durable power of attorney authorizes the representative you name — subject to limitations you establish — to control your assets and manage your financial affairs.

Living Trust

With a living trust, if you become incapacitated, your chosen representative takes over as trustee. A properly drawn living trust avoids guardianship proceedings and related costs, and it offers greater protection and control than a durable power of attorney because the trustee can manage trust assets for your benefit.

Making Health Care Decisions

Two planning techniques to consider regarding making health care decisions while incapacitated are a health care power of attorney and a living will.

Health Care Power of Attorney

A health care power of attorney — also referred to as a "durable medical power of attorney" or "health care proxy" — authorizes a surrogate — your spouse, child or another trusted representative — to make medical decisions or consent to medical treatment on your behalf when you're unable to do so.

Living Will

A living will — also referred to as an "advance health care directive" — expresses your preferences for the use of life-sustaining medical procedures, such as artificial feeding and breathing, surgery, and invasive diagnostic tests. It also specifies the situations in which these procedures should be used or withheld.

Where Do You Go From Here?

Estate planning is an ongoing process. You must not only develop and implement a plan that reflects your current financial and family situation, but also constantly review your current plan. Obviously you need to review and potentially update your plan any time estate tax law changes are signed into law. But there are many other changes that should trigger a review and potentially an update. For example, you'll want to update your plan if there are any changes to your family, such as marriages, divorces, births, adoptions and deaths.

You should also revisit your plan if you encounter any increase in your income and net worth. What may have been an appropriate estate plan when your income and net worth were much lower may no longer be effective today.

Suppose you want to move to a different state. What then? Different states have different laws that could affect your estate plan. So, anytime you move from one state to another, you should review your estate plan.

And don't forget new health-related conditions. For example, you or a child may develop special needs due to physical or mental limitations. Or a surviving spouse's ability to earn a living may change because of a disability.

In such circumstances, it's always a good idea to revisit and update your estate plan to ensure it fits any changes in your circumstances.

If you're like most people, it's easy to put off until tomorrow developing a detailed estate plan — or updating it in light of changes in tax law or your situation. But don't.

Together, we can discuss your situation and help you develop and implement an estate plan that preserves for your heirs what it took you a lifetime to build.

SECTION FIVE

Maximizing Social Security

Introduction

If you have too much money in either of your first two buckets (taxable and tax-deferred) it may cause your Social Security to be taxed. When your Social Security gets taxed, it forces you to spend down your other assets to compensate.

In this section we will cover the following:

- The causes of Social Security taxation

- The definition of Provisional Income

- The Social Security thresholds you need to be aware of

- The real cost of Social Security taxation

- Strategies to reduce or eliminate Social Security taxation[18]

[18] This section presents a general overview of certain rules related to Social Security and the ideas presented are not individualized for your particular situation. This information is based on current law which can be changed at any time.

What is Provisional Income?

To understand why our Social Security gets taxed, it's important to understand "Provisional Income".

Definition: The income the IRS tracks to determine if your Social Security will be taxed.

What Counts as Provisional Income?

1. All earned income

2. Distributions from Qualified Plans (IRAs, 401(k)s, etc.)

3. Required Minimum Distributions (RMDs)

4. 1099s from taxable bucket

5. Pensions

6. Rental income

7. Interest from Municipal Bonds

8. One-half of your Social Security

The IRS adds up all your Provisional Income and, based on that total, and your marital status, determines what percentage of your Social Security benefits will become taxed. That percentage of your Social Security is then taxed at your highest marginal tax rate.

Provisional Income Thresholds (Married Filers)

The provisional income threshold for married couples are as follows:

Provisional Income	Percent of Social Security Subject to Tax
Under $32,000	0%
$32,000 to $44,000	50%
Over $44,000	85%

Provisional Income Thresholds (Single Filers)

The provisional income threshold for Single Filers are as follows:

Provisional Income	Percent of Social Security Subject to Tax
Under $25,000	0%
$25,000 to $34,000	50%
Over $34,000	85%

Example of Social Security Taxation

Bob and Mary's Provisional Income is as follows:

- Pension: $70,000 per year

- Required Minimum Distributions: $30,000 per year

- ½ of Social Security: $15,000 per year

Total Provisional Income: $115,000

Because Bob and Mary breached the $44,000 threshold, 85% of their Social Security becomes taxable at their highest marginal tax bracket.

Assuming a 25% federal tax rate (by the way, most states do not charge state tax for Social Security), and assuming a Social Security benefit of $30,000, then 85% of that amount would be subject to taxation. 85% of $30,000 is $25,500. When we multiply $25,500 by 25%, we find that Bob and Mary's total Social Security tax bill is $6,375 per year!

Social Security Taxation

Because of Social Security taxation, Bob and Mary experienced the following:

- Lost $6,375 in yearly Social Security benefits

- To compensate, they would likely take distributions from their IRA

- At 30% tax rates, this totals $9,107

- Total cost of Social Security Taxation = $9,107 per year!

The Long-Term Costs of Social Security Taxation

The damage doesn't stop here, however. Bob and Mary do lose $9,107 because of Social Security taxation, but they also lose the opportunity cost that goes along with it. What is opportunity cost?

Definition: The cost of an alternative that must be forgone in order to pursue a certain action. Put another way, the benefits you could have received by taking an alternative action.[19]

In other words, when you give up that $9,107, not only do you give up that amount, but you give up what it could have earned for you had you been able to keep it and invest it over the balance of your retirement. If Bob and Mary had been able to keep that $9,107 every year and invest it at 8% over the next 20 years, how much better off could they be? $450,094 better off! So, the total cost of Social Security taxation can take a huge toll on one's retirement over time.

---

[19] Investopedia.com

Social Security Reality Check

In reality, Social Security taxation is much worse than what's been described. How so? Because Social Security rises to keep up with inflation every year. So, you may pay $6,375 in Social Security taxation this year, but next year your Social Security check will be even bigger. The bigger the check, the bigger the tax bill. The bigger the tax bill, the bigger the distribution from your IRA or 401(k) to compensate.

Avoiding Social Security Taxation

Given the realities of Provisional Income, is there any possible way to avoid Social Security taxation? The key is to keep your Provisional Income below the thresholds of which we spoke earlier. This can be done by repositioning a portion of your assets to the tax-advantaged bucket, such that your remaining streams of income keep you below these thresholds. By accumulating the right amounts of money in the right types of accounts, you can reduce Provisional Income to acceptable levels and keep your Social Security free from tax!

Ensure that Your Provisional Income Stays Below Thresholds

Distributions from true tax-advantaged investments do not count as Provisional Income.

What investment accounts qualify as tax-advantaged?

1. Roth IRAs

2. Roth 401(k)s

3. Roth Conversions

4. Some forms of Cash Value Life Insurance

Q: What is the single greatest contributor to Social Security taxation?

A: Having too much money in your:

1. IRAs

2. 401(k)s

3. Pensions, etc.

Reposition tax-deferred assets to tax-advantaged accounts to reduce Provisional Income and avoid Social Security taxation.

Pensions and Social Security Taxation

So, how does all this change if you have a large pension? Remember, 100% of your pension income is counted as Provisional Income. So, if your pension is large enough, it can almost guarantee that your Social Security will be taxable. So, while it's nice to have that guaranteed income in retirement, that income comes at a price.

So, is there any way to get around this? Before making your pension election, explore whether your company offers a lump sum distribution option. This would allow you to roll the lump sum value of your pension into an IRA. And, once it's in an IRA, you could then convert it to a Roth IRA, eliminating it as a source of Provisional Income forever. This may dramatically increase the likelihood that you could get your Social Security free from tax.

In Summary

To this point we have suggested that if tax rates in the future are higher than they are today, then there is a mathematically ideal amount to have in each of the three retirement buckets:

- Taxable Bucket: 6 months' worth of living expenses
- Tax-Deferred Bucket: Balance should be low enough that RMDs at 70 ½ are equal to or less than standard deductions and personal exemptions[20]
- Tax-Advantaged Bucket: Everything above and beyond the ideal balances in the taxable and tax-deferred bucket should be repositioned to tax-advantaged

In this section we also discussed the mechanics of Social Security taxation as well as the impact it may have on your cash flow in retirement. To insulate yourself from the impact of Social Security taxation, you must ensure that your Provisional Income levels stay below the thresholds required by the IRS. This is most easily accomplished by ensuring that you have accumulated the ideal balances in each of the three retirement buckets.

---

[20] When calculating the ideal balance in the tax-deferred bucket, keep in mind that one-half of Social Security counts as Provisional Income. Therefore, these balances may need to be adjusted to stay below minimum Provisional Income thresholds